LATINOS IN BASEBALL

Sammy Sosa

An Authorized Biography

Carrie Muskat

Mitchell Lane Publishers, Inc.
P.O. Box 200
Childs, MD 21916-0200

LATINOS IN BASEBALL

Tino Martinez	Bobby Bonilla	Roberto Alomar	Pedro Martinez
Moises Alou	**Sammy Sosa**	Ivan Rodriguez	Carlos Baerga
Ramon Martinez	Alex Rodriguez	Vinny Castilla	Mariano Rivera

Library of Congress Cataloging-in-Publication Data

Muskat, Carrie
    Sammy Sosa / Carrie Muskat.
      p. cm. —(Latinos in baseball)
    Includes index.
    Summary: Profiles the personal life and professional career of Dominican Republic-born baseball player, Sammy Sosa, who in 1998 broke Roger Maris' home run record along with Mark McGwire.
    ISBN 1-883845-92-0 (lib. bndg.)
    1. Sosa, Sammy, 1968– —Juvenile literature. 2. Baseball players—Dominican Republic—Biography—Juvenile Literature. I. Title. II. Series.
GV865.S59 M87 1999
796.357'092—dc21
[B]

98-54377
CIP
AC

About the Author: Carrie Muskat has covered major league baseball since 1981, beginning with United Press International in Minneapolis. She was UPI's lead writer at the 1991 World Series. A freelance journalist since 1992, she is a regular contributor to *USA Today* and *USA Today Baseball Weekly*. Her work has appeared in the *Chicago Tribune, Inside Sports,* and *ESPN Total Sports* magazine. She is the author of several baseball books for children, including *Barry Bonds* (Chelsea House), *Moises Alou* (Mitchell Lane), and *Mark McQwire* (Chelsea House). She started interviewing and writing about Sammy Sosa when he joined the White Sox in July 1989. She has been to Comiskey Park and Wrigley Field for almost every home game since 1987.

Photo Credits: cover: Sporting News/Archive Photos; p. 4 Jonathan Daniel/Allsport; p. 6 AP Photo; p. 8 Carrie Muskat; p. 13 AP Photo; pp. 18, 20 Carrie Muskat; pp. 39, 41, 44 AP Photo; p. 46 Jonathan Daniel/Allsport; p. 47 Tim Brokema/Allsport; p. 48 Andres Latif/Archive Photos; p. 49 Todd Marcham/Allsport; pp. 53, 54, 55, 56, 57, 58 Carrie Muskat.

Acknowledgments: The following story was developed based on personal interviews with Sammy Sosa from 1989 through 1998. The author has intimate knowledge of the facts contained in this book and has twice been to the Dominican Republic (1996 and 1998) to report on Sammy's life there. This story has been thoroughly researched and checked for accuracy. To the best of our knowledge, it represents a true story.

TABLE OF CONTENTS

Sammy Sosa hits his 62nd home run of the season at Wrigley Field on September 13, 1998

CHAPTER ONE
Sammy Sosa Day

Sunday, September 20, 1998, was the last home game of the regular season for the Chicago Cubs, and it was anything but a normal day.

Wrigley Field was decked out in tricolor Dominican Republic flags. The red, white, and blue flags were flying from the ballpark's roof, from surrounding neighborhood rooftops, and from the front of the fire station across Waveland Avenue behind the left-field bleachers. Merengue music blared from the public-address system. It was sunny, hot, and humid—typical weather for the Dominican Republic, not Chicago in late September.

Early in the day, before the gates to the ballpark opened, Sammy Sosa walked across the bright green outfield to the batting cages that are tucked under the right-field bleachers. He was wearing his lucky T-shirt, which he had altered slightly by cutting off the sleeves. The front of the shirt said: "It's a baseball thing." The back said: "Swing, Hit, Run, Slide, Score."

Cubs manager Jim Riggleman walked with Sosa. Riggleman had a cup of coffee. Sosa had his bat. It was a rare quiet moment for the two. The Cubs were battling for the wild-card spot in the National League playoffs, and Sosa had been hitting home runs at a record-setting pace. It had been a wild, wonderful baseball season in Chicago. Rookie pitcher Kerry Wood tied a major-league record with 20 strikeouts in May. Closer Rod Beck had 50 saves. Sosa had had the most media attention of his teammates and had to entertain many reporters from his native Dominican Republic. Riggleman was under pressure to get the Cubs into the postseason for the first time since 1989.

As Sosa and Riggleman walked across the field, some of the Wrigley Field groundskeepers were attaching a giant-sized banner to the wire fence behind the left-field seats. The sign said: "Sammy: You're the Man." Riggleman had his arm around Sosa's shoulders.

"I was just reminding him to relax and enjoy this last week," Riggleman said later. "I wanted to tell him, 'Through the course of the year, you've been the MVP.'"

It was Sammy Sosa Day at Wrigley Field.

Sammy takes a victory lap around Wrigley field after "Sammy Sosa Day" festivities before the Cubs game against the Cincinnati Reds on Sunday, September 20, 1998, in Chicago.

The Cubs wanted to celebrate Sammy, but not just because he had hit 60-something home runs. The team wanted to salute the 29-year-old outfielder who loves to play baseball and shows it.

Sosa's mother, Lucrecia, was at Wrigley Field for the ceremony along with his brothers, Luis, Juan, and Jose, and his sisters, Sonia and Raquel. Sammy is the second youngest; his older brother, Juan, (1965), spends the summers with Sammy in Chicago. The rest of the family had flown in from the Dominican Republic for the weekend.

Also at the ballpark were Sammy's wife, Sonia, and their four children: six-year-old Keysha; four-year-old Kenia; Sammy Jr., who would turn two on October 26; and little Michael, who had just celebrated his first birthday on September 18. Several Dominican Republic dignitaries were present, plus some 40,000 fans who brought signs and banners honoring Sosa. It was quite a party.

"When I walked outside, I had 3,000 people ask me for tickets," said Manny Alexander, one of Sosa's teammates and a fellow countryman. "We're like the Dominican today."

Practically everyone in the Dominican Republic had followed Sosa's home-run exploits all season long on cable television. Car drivers updated Sosa's totals on their windows, writing No. 61, then 62, then 63. Not only were fans at his games expecting him to hit a home run every time, but so were people on the Caribbean island.

"It comes at a good time," said Fernando Ravelo of Television Dominicana. Ravelo was part of a Dominican Republic crew that had begun broadcasting the Cubs' games on September 11. It was the first time ever that the television station had carried a Major League Baseball game live. Ravelo estimated that eight out of every 10 televisions

Many in the Dominican Republic followed Sammy's home run exploits all season long. Car drivers updated Sammy's totals on their windows.

in the Dominican Republic were tuned to Sosa and the Cubs.

"He's got charisma," Ravelo said of Sosa. "The way he has behaved this year, he's been so unselfish."

Focusing on Sosa helped the island's residents forget for a moment about poverty and brownouts and unemployment. Omar Minaya, assistant general manager of the New York Mets and one of the scouts who originally signed Sosa in 1985, knows how important Sosa is to his countrymen. "Why does Sammy mean so much to them? He gives them hope," Minaya said. "He is a national treasure. He has shown that you can not only become a great player, but you can become a great player with class."

Sosa's special day was a fitting tribute. A five-trumpet fanfare started the pregame festivities. Cubs television broadcaster Chip Caray was the emcee, and he introduced the Sosa family. Sosa's mother, Lucrecia, was wearing a pretty pale yellow dress, while his two daughters were dressed in their lace-trimmed Sunday best.

Also present were Roger Maris's six children. Roger Maris had held the single-season home-run record of 61 set in 1961, but Mark McGwire had broken that mark on September 8. The Maris family was in St. Louis when that happened and had missed Sosa's record-setting efforts on September 13 when he hit home runs No. 61 and 62.

"He always said records were made to be broken," Roger Maris Jr. said of his father, who died in 1985. "I don't think he thought this would last as long as it did."

McGwire had sent a telegram. It read: "Sammy Sosa, congratulations on your special day at Wrigley Field. We have shared an exciting and historic season that will be remembered for years to come. You have handled yourself with class and dignity and are to be commended for a fantastic 1998 season. Enjoy your day."

Major League Baseball commissioner Bud Selig then presented Sosa with the Commissioner's Historic Achievement Award, a crystal trophy (McGwire had also received one). "Your achievements are legendary," Selig said, "but more importantly you've handled yourself with class and dignity that is unparalleled. Your name will forever be linked with Ruth, Aaron, Maris, Ernie Banks, and Billy Williams."

Babe Ruth, Hank Aaron, and Roger Maris were legendary home-run hitters. Ruth hit 60 home runs in

1927, which had been the single-season record until Maris broke it 34 years later. Aaron hit 755 home runs in his career, the most by any ballplayer. Professional Baseball Hall of Famers Ernie Banks and Billy Williams had had tremendous careers with the Cubs. It was an elite group.

Sosa then received certificates from Hall of Fame pitcher Juan Marichal, secretary of sports for the Dominican Republic; and Jose Hazin, a senator from the Dominican Republic.

The Cubs were playing the Cincinnati Reds on this day, and players from both teams were sitting on the grass in front of their respective dugouts to watch the ceremony. They seemed to be the only ones not wearing T-shirts that either spelled out Sosa's name or commemorated his historic home runs.

Cubs general manager Ed Lynch credited Sosa with an "infectious enthusiasm that is an inspiration to all of us, not only in the United States but around the world."

"I can tell you I am proud to have you as my friend," Lynch said.

Riggleman gave Sosa a Tiffany crystal trophy from the team, and Banks, who was waving a small Dominican Republic flag, unveiled a painting of Sosa by artist Malcolm Farley. The team also gave Sosa a purple convertible Chrysler Prowler with the Illinois license plate "Sammy 98."

Lynch then introduced Sosa to the crowd as the "Most Valuable Player in the National League," and Sosa stepped to the microphone, greeted by chants of "MVP, MVP" from the crowd.

"Chicago, I love you," Sosa said.

The fans loved him back, cheering and waving and dancing. Sammy's mother gave him a kiss and a hug and reminded him that he had forgotten to thank his family. Embarrassed, he hurried back to the microphone.

"All I can say," Sosa said, smiling, "is that baseball has been very, very good to me."

He then ran around the field, beginning along the first base side and heading out to right field, his hat in his right hand. He waved to the crowd as the theme from *Superman* played in the background. His sisters hugged each other, and everybody kissed his mother. When Sosa finally arrived in front of the Cubs' dugout, he was engulfed by his teammates in a genuine and heartwarming tribute to their MVP.

"It's been a magical season for Sammy," Riggleman said.

Then, news came that McGwire had just hit home run No. 65 for the St. Louis Cardinals in Milwaukee. McGwire and Sosa had been involved in a friendly rivalry all season. Sosa accepted the news well.

"That's why he's The Man," Sosa said after the game. "I hope he hits 70."

Back to the festivities, Juan Luis Guerra, a popular singer from the Dominican Republic, sang his country's national anthem. It was believed to be the first time ever that the song had been performed before a major-league game in the United States.

Then it was time to play ball. Cincinnati's Reggie Sanders singled to lead off against Cubs pitcher Kevin Tapani. After a 1-0 pitch to Jon Nunnally, the second batter in the first inning, four F-16 jets buzzed the field. Red and blue balloons were let loose behind the left-field bleachers. The timing was off. The jets were supposed to have flown over Wrigley Field after the team took the field.

Tapani ignored the hubbub and calmly threw over to first baseman Mark Grace.

The weather did interrupt the game. Rain fell right before Tapani was to bat in the bottom of the third inning. During the break, the Maris family met with the media to discuss their father's legacy. The 1998 season had been special for the Maris children because there had been so many stories about their father. He had been brought back to life in a positive way. "He's kind of getting his due that he didn't get in '61," Roger Jr. said. The Maris clan certainly enjoyed front-row seats for Sammy Sosa Day. "I don't think anybody in America would miss the chance to see Mark McGwire or Sammy Sosa play baseball," Roger Jr. said.

Michael Jordan was there, too. The NBA superstar watched from a skybox with his Chicago Bulls teammate Scottie Pippen. "I couldn't hit 63 home runs or 64," said Jordan, who in 1994 had retired from basketball to play baseball, only to return to basketball.

Jordan had called Sosa when he had hit home run No. 62 to congratulate him. The first thing Sammy said was, "When are you going to the Dominican Republic?" Jordan promised to visit and play golf.

"He called me," Sosa confirmed after the game, then impishly added, "He called me collect. And I accepted the charge."

The Maris children had one more commitment. After play resumed, they sang "Take Me Out to the Ballgame" during the seventh-inning stretch. The song is a Wrigley Field tradition.

The Cincinnati Reds were terrible guests. Sammy did not hit any home runs, but Bret Boone did, hitting three to lead the Reds to a 7-3 victory over the Cubs. Every one of the 40,117 in attendance wanted to see Sosa homer on his day. Even Sosa did. "I have to say, yes, I was trying to do too much," Sosa said. "Maybe that's one of the reasons I swung at the pitches out of the strike zone."

In his first at-bat in the first, Sosa swung at the first pitch and popped up to first baseman Sean Casey. With one out and two runners on in the third, Sosa struck out swinging against starter Pete Harnisch. He reached first base on an error by Aaron Boone in the fifth but struck out swinging again in the seventh and popped out to Bret Boone to end the game.

Bret Boone called his performance a fluke. Sosa's efforts that season were something close to a miracle. "I can't imagine seeing 60 home runs next to my name," Boone said. "It's something 99.9 percent of us can't fathom doing."

Sammy Sosa did it. But it hadn't been easy.

Sammy flashes his trademark victory sign.

CHAPTER TWO
Shoeshine Boy

S outh of Florida in the Caribbean Sea lies the island of Hispaniola. Two independent countries, the Republic of Haiti and the Dominican Republic, share the island. Christopher Columbus landed on the Dominican Republic side of the island in 1492 in search of gold and silver. Instead, the explorer discovered lots of sun, sand, and palm trees. Columbus moved on, but some 7 million people eventually called the Dominican Republic their home.

Baseball is believed to have been introduced in the Caribbean in 1866 when some U.S. sailors who were in Cuba to transport sugar to America played a game on that island. They invited the Cubans to join them. The game caught on, and Cubans who traveled to the Dominican Republic brought the game with them. Interest caught on, and professional ballclubs were established. The oldest club in the Dominican is Licey, first formed in 1907.

The game received a big boost in the Dominican in the 1940s with the creation of the Mundial, an international championship tournament for amateur baseball. Cuba hosted five consecutive tournaments. The Latin teams dominated the event, and Cuba won 11 out of 18 tournaments from 1940 to 1972. In 1948, the Dominican team won the event just months after almost all of its national championship team had been killed in a plane crash. The tragedy helped pro baseball's rebirth on the island.

The country also established the Dirección General de Deportes, an agency that organizes regional and national tournaments for amateur baseball in the Dominican Republic. Juan Marichal, Manny Mota, and the Alou brothers, Felipe, Matty, and Jesus, all played in these tournaments in the 1950s.

Sugarcane was the biggest business on the island. One of the reasons baseball became so popular in the Dominican was that the sugarcane went through a six-month *tiempo muerte*, or dead season, when the fields required minimal care. With nothing to do, beautiful weather, and plenty of players, baseball became the national sport.

Sugarcane was once the No. 1 export in the Dominican Republic. Some people think today it is baseball players. However, it took Major League Baseball some time before it added Latin players to the rosters. The first African-American player to reach the big leagues was Jackie Robinson in 1947. It was not until 1956 that the first Dominican player made a major-league squad. Ozzie Virgil was the first, playing for the Giants that year. He played all positions except pitcher during his nine big-league seasons. Felipe Alou made his debut two years later, also with the Giants, and he was joined in 1960 first by Marichal, then by Felipe's brother Matty.

Major-league teams sent scouts to the island in search of talent. Some teams established baseball schools in the Dominican Republic. The town of San Pedro de Macoris, located on the southeast end of Hispaniola, became famous for its shortstops. In 1986 there were seven big-league shortstops from that city alone, including Alfredo Griffin, Tony Fernandez, and Rafael Ramirez. San Pedro de Macoris, which has a population of about 100,000 people, sends more of its native sons to the majors on a per capita basis than any other town ever.

In 1979, Bill Chase, a New England native, arrived in the Dominican Republic. Chase was not looking for ballplayers. He was opening three shoe factories in San Pedro de Macoris in what was known as the *zona franca*, or trade-free zone. The location was attractive to him as a businessman. The operating costs were much less expensive in the Dominican than they would have been in the United States.

On his first day in town to open the factory, Chase went to a local park. About 200 kids were there.

"There was this little kid with this big smile," Chase said. "I said to him, 'Do you want to shine my shoes?' He said yes. It was Sammy."

Sammy Sosa was 11 years old at that time. He was living with his mother, Lucrecia, and his three brothers and two sisters in a tiny two-room apartment. Sammy's father, a highway worker, had died at age 42 when Sammy was seven. The family was left to fend for itself, and everyone worked. Sammy shined shoes in the Parque Duarte, a tree-lined square in the center of town. The park was also the center of activity. Motor scooters buzzed around the edge of the park on the dirt roads. Merengue music blasted from the storefronts surrounding the square, and vendors hawked fresh fruit from carts. There was a large legion of shoeshine boys, or *limpia botas*. Sammy and his brothers also sold oranges or washed cars—anything to earn a few extra pesos to help their mother keep food on the table. Sammy often slept on the floor because there wasn't enough room in the bed for all the children. "Being poor was difficult," Sosa's older brother, Juan, said.

Chase liked the wiry boy with the giant smile. Sammy and Juan started to go to the factory every day. Chase kept them busy running errands, acting as messengers, and shining his clients' shoes. "They became part of the family, part of the woodwork," Chase said.

There was one rule that everyone had to adhere to: *No trabajo, no dinero*. That means, "No work, no money." Chase was not going to let the youths freeload off him. They had to earn their pesos.

The boys still went to school, but that only took half a day. In the afternoons they were at the factory, and Chase welcomed them in. The Americans who worked at the plant as supervisors would teach the kids English.

Sammy's mother watched all of this and trusted Chase. "Mother's know," Sammy said. The relationship developed. Whenever Chase and his wife returned home to Miami, Florida, they would collect children's clothes for Sammy and his siblings. In 1981, two years after he had met Sammy, Chase asked the kids if they needed anything. Sammy said he wanted a baseball glove.

Chase had never seen Sammy play, but he had heard about his talent. There was no Little League in the Dominican. Instead, Sammy and his brothers and friends played in the streets, using a rolled-up sock with tape on it for a ball and a stick for a bat. The kids couldn't afford real gloves, so they cut milk cartons in half and used those. If the kids did not have chores to do, they would play baseball all day long.

Dominican kids also play a street game called *vitilla*, using a stick for a bat and a gallon water-bottle cap as a ball. The pitcher throws the cap like a Frisbee; the batter needs good hand-eye coordination and quick reflexes to make contact.

There was a field near Sosa's home that everyone called Mexico. It was a Little League–sized ballpark squeezed into a residential neighborhood of small, one-story pastel-colored cinder-block houses. A prison was located across the street from right field. Alfredo Griffin, Tony

Sammy Sosa grew up in this small house in the Dominican Republic.

Fernandez, George Bell, Juan Samuel, and other Dominicans who made it to the big leagues all played there.

"A lot of people around the factories talked about how [Sammy] was a good player," said Chase, who coaxed one of his plant supervisors to take him to one of Sammy's games. The skinny youth, now 13, was impressive. "He was really hustling out there," Chase said.

Chase wanted to get Sammy a good glove. "He had natural ability," Chase said. "This isn't like America where kids can play in Little League." When Chase got back to the United States, he went shopping and found a glove for $100. It was blue.

Everyone in the Dominican had seen what happened when someone made it to the big leagues. George Bell was from San Pedro de Macoris, and whenever he returned home, he was driving nice cars and wearing expensive clothes and gold jewelry. The same was true for Griffin and Fernandez and Julio Franco. Sammy saw it firsthand. He used to wash Bell's cars and shine the shoes of Pedro Guerrero and Joaquin Andujar.

"Those players, when they came home I saw they had everything," Sammy said. "They had all these people around them. They were like kings. I always said I wanted to be like that."

The message was clear. If you played baseball, you could be rich. "There is no way to make money quickly to help your family unless you are a ballplayer or a singer," Sammy said.

Sammy's brother Luis was a talented ballplayer, and he tried to get a major-league scout interested in signing him. But Luis was too small to make it. Sammy had trained to be a boxer but quit after six months because of his mother. "When I told her, she panicked," he said. "She said if I ever made it, she'd never watch me." Luis recognized Sammy's athletic ability and pushed his younger brother toward baseball. "My brother said, 'Come on, I'm going to put you in the league because you're going to be the one who can make it," Sosa said. "And from there, it just happened." At the age of 14, Sammy started to play organized baseball.

In 1985, Kiki Acevedo, a scout in the Dominican Republic, arranged a tryout in Puerto Plata for some of the young players. Acevedo invited Felipe and Jesus Alou, who were both with the Montreal Expos organization, to check out the young talent.

"[Acevedo] kept telling us about this kid, Samuel Sosa," Felipe Alou said. "[Acevedo] is a guy who signed Julio Franco, Juan Samuel, and George Bell, so if a guy like that tells me he thinks a kid can play, I'm going to go to my grave with his advice."

But Sosa did not impress the Alous. Sammy was six feet tall but a skinny 160 pounds. "All Sammy did was hit weak ground balls to the infield and pop-ups," Jesus Alou said. "All his throws from the outfield were two or three hops." Instead, the Expos signed a pitcher, Mario Brito, and an outfielder, Robinson Dotel.

Amado Dinzey and Omar Minaya, who were scouts with the Texas Rangers, also watched Sammy play. What they saw was a malnourished teen with lots of raw talent. Dinzey had to convince Minaya of this, though. "[Sammy] was not a big kid, but he had an aggressiveness to him—and he had a good arm," Minaya said. "The ball didn't travel far when he hit it but he made good contact. The ball had life when he hit it—that's what impressed me."

Dinzey convinced Minaya to sign Sammy.

"I was young. I thought I was ready," Sammy said. "In my mind, I was ready." On July 30, 1985, Sammy Sosa signed his first professional contract with the Texas Rangers for $3,500.

He was 16 years old.

Sammy and a school boy in the Dominican Republic flash Sammy's "I love you" sign that he gives after home runs.

CHAPTER THREE
Welcome to the U.S.A.

In January 1986, Marty Scott was driving in San Pedro de Macoris, Dominican Republic, with Sandy Johnson and Omar Minaya. Scott was the Texas Rangers director of player development at that time, while Johnson was the team's scouting director and Minaya was a scout. They were looking for Sammy Sosa.

One of the men looked out the car window and saw a street vendor. It was Sammy. He was selling oranges.

"He was just doing anything he could to help the family out," Scott said.

Sosa took the men to his home. There was a front door, but sheets were hung instead of doors to separate the rooms. The floor was concrete.

"I'd heard about his bat speed," Scott said, "but selling oranges on the street corner, you can't tell much about a player's ability. I could see this frail, skinny [guy]. I couldn't see much of a player."

Sosa had signed with the Rangers the previous summer. Minaya could see the potential. "I liked his bat and the way he threw the ball," Minaya said. "I just wasn't sure he could run fast enough."

Sammy's mother was worried about her son. He would be the first to leave the nest. "He said, 'Mama, don't cry. I'm going to make money,'" his brother Juan said.

Sammy had not just his mother's love, he also had a strong religious faith. His belief in God helped him get through the tough times. "She was always praying for her sons," Juan said of his mother. Even though Sammy was going to America by himself, he did not feel he was alone.

His first pro team was the Texas Rangers rookie team in the Gulf Coast League. Sammy had the blue glove that Bill Chase had given him. Minaya was one of the coaches. His teammates included Juan Gonzalez, Rey Sanchez, Kevin Brown, and Dean Palmer.

Playing baseball was easy compared to dealing with life in the United States. Sammy could not speak English. To eat, he would mimic the other players, sometimes eating the same thing every day. If they went to a fast-food restaurant, Sammy would wait until another person ordered and then say, "Like that" and point at a picture of the food. There was no indoctrination program for the Latin ballplayers, not even English classes.

The Rangers did provide nutritional supplements, hoping to erase years of malnourishment. Four or five players would share one apartment and split the $850 monthly rent. By splitting the cost, they were able to send more money home to their families.

"He always had his family in mind," Minaya said. "What he was doing was not only because he liked it but because it was a way for them to escape poverty."

Sammy moved up the next season to Gastonia, where he batted .279. However, he also struck out 123 times in 129 games. He even hit a single on a pitch that bounced before it reached the plate. "He swung at every ball, I think," Scott said. "But his tools were always there—the above-average power, arm, speed. It was just a matter of adjusting to curves in the dirt, hitting to right on outside pitches. I think his most important number was at-bats. He didn't experience great success, and it made him work harder."

Sammy had a great sense of humor. He volunteered to drive the Gastonia team owner's $85,000 Mercedes to an All-Star Game in Charleston, South Carolina. The owner declined. "He was a child when he was here, just 18 years old," said Stevette Harris, who worked in the team's ticket office. "He was real aggressive and playful. He went about playing wholeheartedly, that's what I remember. You could tell he had a lot of personality, but language was a barrier."

Life in the United States was different. Sosa's apartment had a dishwasher, washing machine and dryer, and air conditioner. These were all luxuries to the young Dominican. "We had to make sure they didn't do something like put their cleats in the dishwasher to clean them," said Scott. "But Sammy always had a smile on his face. He wanted to learn."

Some of the families in the Gastonia area invited the players over for dinner. There were never any leftovers from those meals. "Sammy would participate," said Brenda McGinnis, who attended almost every home game from 1980 until 1992, "but you had to take the initiative. A lot of people thought he was temperamental because he'd just stare at you sometimes, but he didn't grasp the language."

Sammy did have one thing going for him, said Jon Robinson, the team's public-address announcer in 1987. "He didn't have great numbers, but he did have a cool name," Robinson said. "*Saaaammy Soooosa.* As an announcer, I loved that."

The young outfielder moved up the next year to Class A Charlotte, where he continued to struggle offensively. Sammy did lead the league in triples with 12, but his strikeouts were still high (106) and his average had dropped to .229.

When Sammy returned home to the Dominican Republic after the 1988 season, he played winter ball for Escogido, a team that was based in the capital city of Santo Domingo. It is an hour's drive from Sammy's home of San Pedro de Macoris to Santo Domingo. Sammy did not have a car. "He had to hitchhike in or get on a bus," said Phil Regan, who was the manager for the Escogido team. "He came to me one day and said he couldn't get back and forth and he was going to have to quit." Regan talked to the team's owner, and soon Sammy had a room at a hotel in Santo Domingo. He no longer had to make the bus ride.

Once he started eating right and getting advice from the Rangers, Sosa also eliminated any doubts about his speed. Regan remembers a time when they inserted Sammy as a pinch runner. "There would be a foul ball and Sammy would be at second base already," Regan said. "You just said, 'Wow.' He was raw, but he was exciting and he had a great personality. He was always smiling."

Escogido won the Caribbean World Series that year and each player received 1,200 pesos, or about $300. Regan asked Sammy what he was going to do with the cash. "My mother gets this money," Sammy said.

Regan, who later managed the Baltimore Orioles and was the Chicago Cubs pitching coach, was dazzled by Sosa. "An outstanding kid. Great attitude," Regan told the *Chicago Tribune* in 1989. "Really hungry and wants to learn. The manager will never have a problem with him. He reminds me of [Roberto] Clemente. He's built like Clemente and runs like Clemente. I don't know if he's going to be another Clemente, but he's got a chance to be a very good major-league player."

The Rangers bumped Sammy up to the Class-AA level at the beginning of 1989 and he started the year in

Tulsa. He batted .297 with seven homers, his best average in the minor leagues, and was called up to the big-league team that year. On June 16, 1989, Sosa made his major-league debut against the New York Yankees. He had two hits, his first coming off Andy Hawkins. Five days later, on June 21, Sosa hit his first major-league home run off Boston's hard-throwing right-hander Roger Clemens.

Sammy lasted about a month in the majors, batting .238, and on July 20 he was optioned to Class AAA Oklahoma City. He did not fare well, going 4 for 39 (.103) in 10 games.

Sosa and pitcher Wilson Alvarez were highly regarded prospects in the Rangers minor-league system. The Rangers also had another talented young outfielder in Juan Gonzalez in the minors.

Larry Himes was the general manager of the Chicago White Sox in 1989. He had heard about Sosa and went to Oklahoma City to watch him play for four days. Sammy had gained some weight and muscle since he first broke in—he was now 170 pounds—and was playing right field. He was still struggling at the plate. "He was above average, a good runner, an outstanding arm," Himes said. "The thing that made him stand out was that when batting practice was over, Sammy had a little net and a little batting tee and a bag of balls. There wasn't anybody on the field and the rest of his team was in the clubhouse. He was out in front of the clubhouse. We watched him. He took one ball, put it on the tee and whacked it. He did this for 20 minutes."

The second day, Sosa went through the same routine. By himself. No coach was goading him on and no manager was yelling. "You get a guy with that type of energy and desire—that's what you want," Himes said.

On July 29, the White Sox traded outfielder and designated hitter Harold Baines and infielder Fred Manrique to the Texas Rangers for Sosa, Alvarez, and infielder Scott Fletcher.

At the time, the deal seemed good for the Rangers. Baines would fit well into the lineup with Rafael Palmeiro, Julio Franco, and Ruben Sierra. Sportswriter Jim Reeves wrote in the *Fort Worth Star-Telegram*, "By making the trade, the Rangers showed their fans, and more importantly, their players, that they're willing to do what it takes to keep the team in the pennant race down the stretch."

Baines was a favorite in Chicago. "It's an unpopular decision as far as the fans are concerned, but sometimes unpopular means exactly that—unpopular," Himes said at the time. "This is a decision we made as far as the direction of the Chicago White Sox for today and for our future."

Once the deal was completed, Sosa was assigned to the White Sox's Triple-A team in Vancouver. He hit an impressive .367 in 13 games. Himes had guessed that Sosa would be called up in September when major-league teams are allowed to expand their rosters, but the young outfielder was in the big-league club even sooner. He made his White Sox debut on August 22 against Minnesota and went 3 for 3 with a home run, two RBIs, and two runs scored as Chicago beat the Twins 10-2. "Nice debut, huh?" White Sox manager Jeff Torborg said.

Sosa walked in his first two at-bats, led off the fifth with a single to center, and grounded a single to left in the seventh. In the ninth, he hit a line-drive homer that landed in the left-field seats at the Metrodome.

"That'll happen to a kid—can't handle the pressure," Torborg said jokingly.

"Pressure? For what?" Sosa said.

"That's Sammy," Fletcher said. "He's probably not going to get three hits every game, but Sammy's a good player. He can run, throw, hit, hit with some power. And he's going to get better."

"He's a little rough around the edges, that's all," said Marv Foley, the Vancouver manager who had Sosa for two weeks before his debut. "But he's got the potential to be a great one. I would say in three years, Sammy's going to be a front-line major-league player.

"There's no telling what he could do."

CHAPTER FOUR
Big Leagues, Big Adjustment

S ammy Sosa made a good first impression with the Chicago White Sox. In his first 13 games, he batted .340 with two homers and four stolen bases. He finished the 1989 season with a .273 average in 33 games. Sosa did make mistakes. He had an outstanding arm but missed throwing to the cutoff man on a couple of plays. "He's just getting comfortable on this level," White Sox manager Jeff Torborg said.

Veteran White Sox catcher Carlton Fisk recognized the young outfielder's potential. "He can run, he throws, he's strong, young. Maybe he's fortunate to be with this organization, so that he gets a chance right off," Fisk said. "As long as he realizes he still has a lot to learn, and wants to learn and has the ability to learn, he's got a chance to be a pretty good player."

Sosa's skills did need some polishing, and he knew that. "I need to work hard every day on everything," he said. "In baseball, you need to work hard every day, day by day."

He had spent most of his minor-league career in right field, and the White Sox were considering moving him to center. Sosa was willing to play anywhere—left, right, or center. During spring training 1990, Torborg decided to go with Lance Johnson in center and put Sammy and his strong arm in right field. "You've got to take advantage of that arm," Torborg said.

But the 1990 season was a struggle for Sosa. It was his first full year in the big leagues and also his first year under the tutelage of White Sox hitting coach Walt Hriniak. Sosa did not adjust well.

"We'd fight, a couple of times," Sosa said later of his verbal battles with the White Sox coach. "He's a pretty good guy, good to work with. But everybody cannot be the same guy. I had to deal with it because I was a young guy. I was scared they were going to send me to Triple-A."

Sosa was the only American League player that season to reach double figures in doubles (26), triples (10), homers (15) and steals (32). But he hit .233 and struck out 150 times in 153 games.

He also had made 13 errors in his first full season, so he concentrated on improving his defensive play as well. "Last year was my first full year, and I was thinking when somebody hit a ground ball to me in the outfield, I've got to go hard and cut the ball off, get a good jump to throw the ball to home plate," he said. "This year is going to be better for me."

But the 1991 season was worse. Sosa started the year well, hitting two homers and driving in five runs on Opening Day in Baltimore. It went downhill after that. Sosa was taken out of the starting lineup for the first time on April 22. A few days later, he met with Torborg behind closed doors. Sosa had requested the meeting. "He knew he was struggling, and he just wanted to know what my thoughts were at the time," Torborg said of Sosa, who was hitting .150 at that point.

Sammy did not think he could get better unless he played. Torborg explained that he sometimes altered his lineup because scouting reports project another player will have better success against a particular team.

The power was there. Twice in May he won games with 12th-inning home runs, including a blast May 10 to help the White Sox beat the Toronto Blue Jays 5-3 before a sellout crowd of 50,198 at SkyDome. But in June, he slipped back into an offensive funk. "It's part of the game," Sosa said after hitting .173 for the month. "I'm working every day with Walt Hriniak on doing what I have to do—keeping my head down and seeing the ball."

The White Sox sent him down to their Triple-A Vancouver team July 19 through August 27. Sosa was hitting .200 when he was demoted. When he rejoined the major-league team, he was convinced he had made the adjustment. "This time I'll stay here forever," he said. "This time I'm a better man and I'll do a better job."

He ended that season batting .203 in 116 games. It was frustrating because he knew he could do better but felt Hriniak's coaching style restricted him. Himes had left the White Sox after the 1990 season and joined their crosstown rivals, the Chicago Cubs, as general manager. He had kept his eye on Sosa and felt he knew what was wrong.

"I thought he had outstanding ability and I felt he was tied into something [Hrniak's style] that was difficult for him to adjust to," Himes said. "I felt [Sosa] was suffering over there from being confined and restricted in his approach to hitting. I've always liked what he could do running, what he could do throwing. He showed me power."

White Sox manager Gene Lamont visited Sammy in the Dominican Republic during the off-season, which was a busy one for Sosa. He married Sonia Esther in November 1991. The two had met a few years earlier at a dance club in Santo Domingo.

Sammy was encouraged by his talk with Lamont, even though the White Sox manager was projecting a platoon in the outfield. "We always talk about his potential and everything, but he needs to play like everybody says he can," Lamont said. In baseball, *to platoon* is to alternate two players in the same position.

Himes had traded for the young outfielder once. On March 30, 1992, just one week before the regular season was to start, he traded for Sosa again. This time he sent veteran outfielder George Bell—whose cars Sosa had washed when he was a kid in their native Dominican—to the White Sox in exchange for Sosa and relief pitcher Ken Patterson. It was only the second deal involving the Cubs and White Sox in a decade.

"We traded top-notch, quality guys for him," Himes said, speaking of Bell and Harold Baines. "George was a professional hitter with power, but he wasn't a National League guy. Sammy was a National League guy."

Sosa's performance so far in the majors—he was a career .228 hitter—left Himes open to criticism for making the move. He was willing to take that risk. "Sammy had the energy and the desire," Himes said. "He had more energy than our whole Cub team when he came over."

Sosa welcomed the trade. "What happened in the first couple of years in Chicago [with the White Sox] was they said I was a selfish player because I wanted to do everything for myself," he said. "That's not right. When you pay somebody, you want that guy to do everything for you, right? So you're not going to pay a guy, when you have a man on second and a man on third, to take a walk. You know what I mean? When the pressure's on, I'm the man. I want to be there."

"He's got a lot of talent," White Sox general manager Ron Schueler said. "One of these years, he's going to put it all together."

Sammy hoped he would get that chance with the Chicago Cubs.

CHAPTER FIVE
30-30

In 1992, the Chicago Cubs already had a very good right fielder in Andre Dawson. He had won the National League Most Valuable Player award in 1987 when he led the league with 49 home runs and 137 RBIs. Cubs manager Jim Lefebvre decided to play Sammy Sosa in center field to take advantage of his speed.

Unfortunately, Sammy's first year with the Cubs was hampered by injuries. His struggles at the plate carried over to the start of the season. Sosa hit just .211 in his first 24 games with one RBI, and that one RBI came on Opening Day. He drove in his second run on May 5, and two days later he hit his first Cubs homer off Houston's Ryan Bowen. On June 10, Sammy posted his second career two-homer game at St. Louis. But in his next game, Montreal's Dennis Martinez hit Sosa with a pitch, breaking a finger in his right hand. Sammy was sidelined June 13 through July 27.

He came back strong. In his first at-bat after being activated from the disabled list, Sosa faced Pittsburgh pitcher Doug Drabek. Sammy homered on the first pitch he saw. The hand had apparently healed well. Sammy went 15 for 39 in his first nine games back, hitting three homers and driving in nine runs.

But in the first inning of the 10th game after his return, Sosa fouled a pitch off his left ankle. He fell to the ground in pain and stayed there for several minutes. Somehow, Sammy got to his feet and stayed in the batter's box long enough to draw a walk, but then he asked to come out of the game. It was first believed he had suffered a bad bruise, but preliminary X rays after the game revealed a fracture. He had broken the large protruding bone on his left ankle. "To me, it was a one-in-a-million freak accident," team trainer John Fierro said. Sammy missed the remainder of the season because of the injury.

Heading into the 1993 season, Cubs general manager Larry Himes and Lefebvre had one wish for the team: Stay healthy. Dawson was gone, having departed via free agency to the Boston Red Sox. That meant right field was open and waiting for Sosa.

"Everybody knows who Andre Dawson was," Sosa said. "The only reason he's not playing in right field is because he's not here. The fans know what I can do. I'm Sammy Sosa."

Sammy showed them what he could do in 1993. He became the first player in Cubs history to record a 30-homer, 30-stolen-base season. He compiled a .261 batting average with 33 homers and 36 stolen bases. His year included a 6-for-6 game on July 2 at Colorado, the first by any Cubs player since Jose Cardenal did so in May 1976. During the week June 28-July 4, Sosa batted .538 in six games with two homers and six RBIs.

Sosa worked hard, but he also had some help. Billy Williams, a Hall of Fame outfielder with the Cubs, was the team's batting coach. He was old-fashioned, and unlike Sosa's coach with the White Sox, Walt Hriniak, he did not believe in dramatically altering a player's swing.

In Sosa, Williams saw a player with an unconventional—and uncomfortable—swing. Early in his Cubs career, Sosa would look into the dugout after every pitch. Williams was confused. "I told him, 'Hey, look at the pitcher. That's the guy trying to get you out,'" Williams said. Hriniak had drilled the dugout reflex into Sosa. "What happened to me happened to everybody over there," Sosa said of the White Sox. "[Hriniak] changed them. You see how everybody's got to look, keep their head down. I don't have to worry about that anymore. [Williams] told me, he said, 'Hey, you're not a Chicago White Sox anymore. Just go out there and do what you can do.'"

Hriniak had helped many major-league players be successful, but Sammy Sosa needed to hit like Sammy Sosa.

"What we tried to do with Sammy," said Tony Muser, "is basically what everybody's tried to do and that is shorten his swing and make him a little better contact-conscious, use more of the baseball field, right center, left center, don't try to pull too much." Muser, a former hitting instructor who was on the Cubs coaching staff, gave Williams a lot of the credit because of the time and energy he devoted to Sosa. "Sammy's done the work and the credit goes to Sammy," Muser said, "but Billy Williams has been the quiet, consistent mentor."

Williams would talk to Sosa not just at the batting cage but also on the team bus rides and on the charter flights between ballparks and in the clubhouse. "Billy has never, ever had one bad thing to say about Sammy and he's realized his potential," Muser said. "I think all of us need that. Everybody else thinks you can't. But Billy always said, 'You can.'"

Sosa followed his stellar 1993 season with another solid year in 1994. He won the Cubs' "triple crown," batting a career-high .300 with 25 homers and 70 RBIs. He also led the team with 22 stolen bases. That season was cut short by a players' strike on August 12, which resulted in the cancellation of the postseason and the World Series.

When play resumed in 1995, the Cubs had a new manager in Jim Riggleman. In April, the team signed Sosa to a new $4.3 million contract, tops on the team. Sammy responded well. He posted his second 30-30 season and became the first Cubs player in the 20th century to lead the team in homers (36) and steals (34) in three consecutive seasons. Sosa tied for second in the National League in home runs and for the league lead in games played (144). For the first time in his career, he was named to the All-Star team.

"Our expectations are so high for him that there is no way he can live up to everybody's expectations on a daily basis," Riggleman said. "But he does put together those long stretches when he does some phenomenal things."

During a 13-game span from August 17 to August 30, Sammy hit 10 homers, including seven in seven games. The only other Cub to hit 10 home runs in that amount of time was Hack Wilson in 1928.

In 1996, Sosa definitely had his power stroke going for him. On May 5 he broke a window in an apartment building across Waveland Avenue from Wrigley Field with a home run. He was leading the National League with 40 home runs when he was hit by a pitch by Florida's Mark Hutton with the bases loaded at a home game on August 20. A run scored on the play, Sosa's 100th RBI of the year, but it also was his last for that season. He stayed in the game for four innings and finally left because of the pain. X rays showed a clean break of a bone on the outside of his right hand near the hand and wrist juncture. He was lost for the year.

"It was the most disappointing news I've gotten in my professional career," Cubs general manager Ed Lynch said. "You come to take Sammy for granted."

"Do we have a 40-home-run guy to replace him? Absolutely not," Cubs first baseman Mark Grace said.

"I have to take it like a man. This isn't the end to my career," Sosa said. "I'll come back. [The Cubs have] got to keep going just like I was in the lineup."

He spent the remainder of the '96 season watching from the bench. It was an uncomfortable seat. "When I was hurt, I was like a kid," Sammy said. "I'd go there, watch the games and do nothing. I hope that never happens to me again."

So did the Cubs. If the team ever wanted to reach the postseason, which had not happened since 1989, it needed a healthy Sammy Sosa.

The off-season was a joyous one. Sammy's wife, Sonia, gave birth to the couple's third child and first son, Sammy Jr., on October 26, 1996. Sammy Sr. arrived for spring training with his hand healed and ready to go. He was now 200 muscle-packed pounds.

In 1997 the Cubs got off to a horrendous 0-14 start in April, and Sosa hit just .216 for the month. "The way I play the game, sometimes I try to hit two home runs in one at-bat," Sosa said.

May was different. Sammy drove in a career-high 6 runs May 16 against San Diego, going 4 for 4 with a homer and a triple. On May 18 he posted his 22nd career multi-homer game against San Francisco. Against Pittsburgh on May 26, he dashed around the bases for his first inside-the-park home run in the top of the sixth. Coincidentally, the Pirates' Tony Womack hit an inside-the-park home run of his own moments later. It was the first time in almost 11 years that two such homers were hit in the same game.

Sosa finished the year ranked among the National League's best with 36 home runs and 119 RBIs, which equaled his career best. However, he also struck out 174 times, tops in the league.

Sammy did not miss a game, playing all 162. In the National League, only Houston's Craig Biggio and Jeff Bagwell and Los Angeles' Eric Karros appeared in every game. And Sosa started all but one game, and that was the season finale September 28 at St. Louis.

He now had 207 home runs in his career—No. 200 had come August 24 off Montreal's Steve Kline—and 1,088 hits. His 1,000th had been a single August 20 off Florida's Livan Hernandez, and it had come on the one-year anniversary of his hand injury.

The biggest day of Sosa's 1997 season came June 27. Cubs chief executive officer Andy MacPhail called an impromptu news conference in the back of the press box at Wrigley Field. MacPhail wanted to announce that the Cubs had signed Sammy to a four-year, $42.5 million contract. The deal made Sosa the third-highest-paid player in baseball. San Francisco's Barry Bonds was first with an annual salary of $11.45 million, followed by Albert Belle of the Chicago White Sox at $11 million. The average yearly salary for Sosa's contract was $10.65 million.

"People always talk about the millions of dollars," Sosa said. "This is not my type of thing. Money doesn't mean anything to me. The only reason I'm here is because I play good."

"I think Sammy deserves this because of the contributions he has made over the past few years," MacPhail said.

Sammy's first hit after signing the deal came the next day: a two-run homer. "After you have the opportunity to sign a contract like that, people are looking for you to hit three- or four-run homers every day," Sosa said.

He couldn't do that. But in 1998, he gave those people a year to remember.

CHAPTER SIX
"Believe It"

J ust a few days into spring training in 1998, on February 18, the Chicago Cubs were saddened by the news that longtime broadcaster Harry Caray had died. The 1998 season would have been Caray's 54th for broadcasting major-league baseball and his 17th with the Cubs. He was 84 when he died. Sammy Sosa, first baseman Mark Grace, and manager Jim Riggleman represented the team at the funeral in Chicago. The gravelly voiced, silver-haired broadcaster did not just call the plays, he loved the Cubs. Caray's grandson Chip was to begin broadcasting games with his grandfather; instead he inherited Harry's seat in the booth.

There was another change. Jeff Pentland was the new Cubs hitting coach. In spring training, he and Sosa continued extra hitting sessions in the batting cages. Pentland would get down on one knee or sit and throw underhand to Sammy from close range to get him to slow down his swing. By being more deliberate at the plate, he would have more time to read and recognize a pitch. Their code word was *suave*, which is Spanish for "smooth."

"One of his goals was to hit .300," Pentland said. "My goals to him were to score 100 runs and walk 100 times. He added the third one." Pentland and Sosa did not discuss reducing the number of strikeouts. That would come if Sosa could develop patience at the plate. They also did not talk about home runs.

The Cubs lost on Opening Day, an 11-6 decision to Florida, but won their next six games. Included in the victories was Sosa's first home run on April 4 off Montreal's Marc Valdes. Sammy hit six homers in the first month and, more importantly, batted .343. He had started the year a career .257 batter and had hit .300 in only one season, so the high percentage was a surprise. Sosa, striving to be a more complete player, matched his April numbers with a .344 mark in May.

At the end of May, Sammy had 13 home runs. Mark McGwire, the powerful first baseman on the St. Louis Cardinals, had 27. The major-league record for the most home runs in a single season was 61, set in 1961 by Roger Maris. Maris had broken Babe Ruth's record of 60, set in 1927, and they were the only ballplayers to ever hit 60 in one season. Because McGwire was off to such a hot start, he was projected to become the third.

No one could have predicted Sammy Sosa's June.

In June 1998, Sammy hit one home run after another.

On June 1, in Sosa's first at-bat of the month, he homered off Florida's Ryan Dempster. He added another blast later in the game to raise his season total to 15. From June 3 to 8, he homered in five straight games, then clubbed five more over a three-game span from June 19 to 21. He hit his 33rd homer in his last at-bat of June off Arizona's Alan Embree. All told, Sammy hit 20 homers in the month, establishing a major-league record. The old mark was 18 set by Detroit's Rudy York in August 1937.

"It's just so much fun to watch him," Pentland said of Sosa. "It's not supposed to be that easy."

Sammy totaled 21 homers in a 30-day period from May 25 to June 23, the most during any 30-day span in major-league history. The home-run chase was getting interesting. By the end of June, McGwire had 37 homers. Sosa had 33.

"Mark McGwire is in a different world," Sosa said. "He's my idol. He's the man."

Sosa was not interested in erasing any records. "If I try [to hit a home run], I'll never get it because I'll overswing," he said. "I only go out there to try to make contact and forget about home runs. When I make good contact, the ball is going to jump anyways."

Despite all his home runs, the Cubs went 12 for 15 in June and were seven games behind first-place Houston. Sammy had a job to do to keep his team in contention.

He did not continue his hot home-run pace in July—he totaled nine—but it was a historic month for Sosa. On July 27 at Arizona, Sammy hit a two-run homer, his 39th, in the sixth inning off Willie Blair. The game was tied 2-2. The Cubs loaded the bases in the eighth and Sosa was up. He had hit 246 career home runs, but he had never hit a grand slam.

Sammy stepped in against Alan Embree. The crowd of 47,753, including many Cubs fans, was cheering. Sosa slugged the first pitch high into the picnic area in right-center field for his first career grand slam. The Cubs won 6-2.

The next day, Sosa came to bat again with the bases loaded in the fifth against Arizona's Bob Wolcott. And again, Sammy homered, clearing the left-field wall. He had two grand slams in four at-bats after not hitting one in his first 4,428 major-league at-bats.

"It's always hard when you're trying to do the first one," Sosa said. "After the first one, you get that out of the way, the pressure is off. The other one, you're not even wait-

St. Louis Cardinal first baseman Mark McGwire blows a trademark Sammy Sosa kiss to the Chicago slugger after Sosa was walked in the seventh inning in Chicago, Wednesday, August 19, 1998. Sosa and McGwire both hit their 48th home runs of the season during the game.

ing for. It was just there." Sammy became the 16th major-leaguer to hit a grand slam in consecutive games.

Sammy trailed McGwire 45-43 going into a three-game series August 7-9 between the Cubs and Cardinals at St. Louis. There would be plenty of hoopla surrounding the showdown between baseball's big hitters. McGwire was not enjoying all the media attention. "It's probably been a little bit aggravating to him, all the reporters bothering him. Every day, every day, every day," said Sosa, who seemed to bask in the spotlight. "I'm enjoying it. Believe me," Sammy said.

Cubs-Cardinals games are always festive events because of the intense rivalry between the fans of the two teams. St. Louis romped 16-3 in the series opener and neither Sosa nor McGwire homered. The next day was a thriller. St. Louis opened a 5-3 lead, aided by McGwire's 46th home run. Sosa tied it 5-5 with a two-run homer in the ninth, his 44th, to force extra innings. The two teams exchanged runs in the 11th and again in the 12th. In the Cardinals' 13th, McGwire came up with two runners on base. The largest Busch Stadium crowd of the year—48,064—was on its feet. McGwire did not get a chance and was intentionally walked to load the bases. Ray Lankford then hit an RBI single to give St. Louis a 9-8 win. "They kept coming and kept coming," Sosa said of the Cardinals. "It was like a World Series for us and for them."

In that game, Sosa was more proud of his 12th-inning RBI single than his home run. "Last year, in that last at-bat, I probably [would have struck] out, I [would have gone] for the three-run homer," he said. "That at-bat meant more to me than anything because it was more professional than just home-run hitting."

The Cubs tried to change their luck before the series finale. Players swapped jerseys with each other. Shortstop Jeff Blauser was wearing Sosa's No. 21. "I just wanted to wear Sammy's jersey for a day and see what it felt like," Blauser said. The Cubs put their regular jerseys back on for the game, but their luck hadn't changed. The Cardinals won 2-1 for the sweep.

Sosa did pull even with McGwire one day later, hitting two home runs against San Francisco to raise his total to 46. McGwire responded the next day by hitting No. 47.

They faced off again August 18-19 at Wrigley Field, and this time they were tied with 47 each. The Cubs won the first game 4-1, and Sosa and McGwire were a combined 0 for 9. The next day, Sammy homered off St. Louis pitcher Kent Bottenfield in the fifth inning to temporarily take the lead with 48 home runs. His lead lasted less than an hour. In the eighth, McGwire hit a solo homer and added an exclamation point when he hit the game-winner in the 10th. St. Louis won 8-6. "That's why he is The Man," Sosa said of McGwire.

The two entered the final month tied at 55. Their home-run heroics had captivated baseball fans across the country. An explosion of flashbulbs followed every Sosa and McGwire at-bat at every ballpark they played as people tried to capture a piece of history.

The National League record for most home runs in a single season was 56 set by Hack Wilson of the Cubs in 1930. McGwire got there first, hitting Nos. 56 and 57 on September 1 and adding Nos. 58 and 59 the next day. Sosa reached 56 on September 2 off Cincinnati's Jason Bere. Coincidentally, a picture and story about Wilson hang next to Sosa's locker in the Cubs' clubhouse.

Fans of Sammy Sosa react when Sosa came to bat Tuesday, August 25, 1998, against the Cincinnati Reds. Sosa had three hits, but no home runs in the game won by the Reds, 10-9.

McGwire and Sosa would meet once more September 7-8 in St. Louis. McGwire had 60 home runs; Sosa had 58. The Cardinals had issued about 700 media credentials for the two-game series, typical for a World Series game but not for a regular-season contest. Roger Maris's six children were in the stands, along with Major League Baseball officials. The St. Louis fans showed their admiration for Sosa's efforts and gave him a standing ovation before his first at-bat, which is unheard of for a visiting player.

McGwire got the loudest cheers. In the Cardinals' first, he tied Maris with a home run off the Cubs' Mike Morgan. Sammy tucked his glove under his arm and applauded "Big Mac" from his position in right field.

The next day, McGwire broke the record with a hit off Chicago's Steve Trachsel, hitting No. 62. Sosa raced in from right field to hug the giant-sized redhead after the homer. "I'm glad that I was here," Sosa said.

Sammy's fans were glad he was in Chicago for a wild weekend September 11-13. He hit home run No. 59 on September 11 and clubbed No. 60 the next day against Milwaukee. On Sunday, September 13, before a standing-room-only crowd of 40,846, the largest of the year at Wrigley Field, Sosa hit Nos. 61 and 62.

Homer No. 61 came in the fifth inning when Sammy launched an 0-1 pitch from Milwaukee's Bronswell Patrick 480 feet over the left-field bleachers. In the ninth, he sent a 2-1 pitch from Eric Plunk over the same seats, and it was measured at the same distance. The 62 homers put Sosa in elite company. "Babe Ruth was one of the greatest guys to play baseball," Sosa said. "Babe Ruth is still alive. He never died. Everybody remembers Babe Ruth like it was yesterday. I feel great to be there with Babe Ruth, Roger Maris, and Mark McGwire."

Sosa climbed to the top step of the Cubs' dugout and doffed his cap twice after hitting No. 62. When the crowd started to chant "MVP, MVP," he took a third curtain call. "For the first time, I was so emotional," Sammy said. "No. 61 reminded me a lot of Mark McGwire in St. Louis. When I got 62, it was something unbelievable. I can't believe what I'm doing."

His teammates knew how special it was and carried Sosa off the field on their shoulders after the game, which the Cubs had won 11-10 in 10 innings.

At 62, Sosa was again tied with McGwire. "Do you think he's waiting for me?" Sammy joked.

It was back to reality the next game, September 14, at San Diego. Sosa struck out four times for the first time all season as the Cubs lost 4-3 to the Padres. Earlier in the day, Sosa had received phone calls from President Bill Clinton and from McGwire. "He [Clinton] congratulated

Sammy hit his 62nd home run at Wrigley field in front of a sellout crowd plus many fans who watched from nearby rooftops.

me and everything. He said he's a Chicago Cubs fan. He told me he wanted me to take the Cubs to the playoffs. I said, 'I'll do my very best,'" Sosa said. McGwire also encouraged him. "He called me and congratulated me and told me to keep going," Sammy said. "I said, 'Same to you.' Let's see how it goes."

Sosa kept going. On September 16, he connected on his third grand slam of the season off San Diego's Brian Boehringer. He added two more homers off Milwaukee on September 23 in his 11th multi-homer game of the year. Two days later in Houston, Sosa launched a 462-foot drive into the third level of the Astrodome for No. 66 and took the lead over McGwire, who had 65. But McGwire, who was playing in St. Louis that night against Montreal, answered 45 minutes later with his 66th.

"Disappointed? For what? Mark is my friend, not my enemy," Sosa said after the game.

McGwire's season ended with 70 home runs. Sammy's season went into overtime.

Sammy celebrates his 62nd home run.

All year, Sammy had tried to deflect the attention he was getting by saying that reaching the playoffs was more important than winning the home-run race. The Cubs finished the regular season 90-73 and tied with San Francisco for the National League wild-card spot, forcing a one-game playoff at Wrigley Field. The winner would advance to the division series against Atlanta. The loser would go home.

"One more day to put on the hard hat, get out the lunch pail, and clock in," Grace said.

The one-game playoff was the National League's first since 1980. The 39,556 fans at a chilly Wrigley Field cheered every pitch. The Giants kept Sosa in check, limit-

Sammy celebrates with his teammates after the Cubs defeated the Houston Astros 3–2 at the Astrodome, September 26, 1998.

ing him to two singles in four at-bats, but unlikely heroes Steve Trachsel, Gary Gaetti, and Matt Mieske combined to give the Cubs a 5-3 victory. It was a team effort. Trachsel pitched well for the win, Gaetti hit a fifth-inning homer, and Mieske came through with a two-run pinch-hit single in the sixth. For the first time since 1989, Chicago was in the playoffs. The Cubs celebrated by dousing each other with champagne.

Unfortunately for the Cubs, they could not advance past the talented pitching staff of the Atlanta Braves, who swept the best-of-five National League Division Series. Atlanta clinched it with a 6-2 victory at Wrigley Field October 3.

Sammy signs autographs at Qualcomm Stadium in San Diego, California, on September 14, 1998.

Sammy did not want to leave the ballpark without saying good-bye to his faithful following. The Cubs came back onto the field for one final curtain call, and Sosa went out to right field to salute the bleacher fans. "They [the fans] all deserve a big hug," Gaetti said. Sosa got just two hits in 11 at-bats in the brief three-game series.

"If I could have given my life to get us to the World Series," Sammy said, "I would have."

The 1998 baseball season might have been the best ever. McGwire finished with his 70, the New York Yankees won 114 games (two short of the 1906 Cubs' all-time record), and Sammy Sosa drove in a league-leading 158 runs. Cubs rookie pitcher Kerry Wood tied a major-league record by striking out 20 in a game in May, while Baltimore's Cal Ripken Jr. ended his consecutive games played streak at 2,632. Seattle's Alex Rodriguez became the third player ever to post a 40-40 season with 42 homers and 46 stolen bases. David Wells pitched a perfect game for the Yankees. For the first time ever, four players finished with 50 home runs—McGwire, Sosa, Ken Griffey Jr., and Greg Vaughn.

To wrap up the season, Sammy won the National League MVP in November. He received 30 of the 32 first-place votes and a total of 438 points in the balloting by the Baseball Writers' Association of America. Mark McGwire garnered second place and Moises Alou took third.

It was unbelievable.

"Believe it," Sosa said.

CHAPTER SEVEN
Sammy Claus

Roberto Clemente is a hero to Latin ballplayers. The Puerto Rican was considered one of the greatest outfielders of the 1960s and won four batting titles with the Pittsburgh Pirates. In the final game of the 1972 season, Clemente garnered his 3,000th hit. He was respected for his humanitarian efforts, too. On New Year's Eve 1972, Clemente was flying with food and medical supplies to help Nicaraguan earthquake victims. The plane crashed, killing him and ending his career much too soon. Because of the circumstances of his death, the Professional Baseball Hall of Fame waived its usual five-year waiting period, and Clemente became the first Latin player inducted into Cooperstown.

Clemente wore No. 21 with the Pirates, and many Latinos in the major leagues consider it an honor to don that number. When Sammy Sosa played for the Chicago White Sox, he wore No. 25, but he was often compared to Clemente, especially in the strength of his arm. Upon joining the Chicago Cubs in 1992, Sosa was assigned No. 21.

Maybe the Cubs were thinking about Clemente when they did it.

"I always say if you want to compare me to Roberto Clemente, I'll be happy," Sammy said. "But I'll never forget that I'm Sammy Sosa. I'm me. Roberto Clemente is a Hall of Famer. I say to myself, Roberto had the arm, he can hit, he can do everything. I'm trying to put my name there, too. Roberto had his time. Now is my time. I want people to never forget me like they never forget Roberto Clemente."

The two share more than a number and gifted athletic ability. Sammy also has a big heart.

In 1996, Sosa financed construction of the $1.2 million 30-30 Plaza in his hometown of San Pedro de Macoris. Building the three-story office complex provided jobs for people. A medical clinic was established there. Sammy's two sisters, Raquel and Sonia, run a beauty salon and a boutique in the building. The 30-30 name is because of Sosa's two 30-30 seasons with the Cubs when he reached 30 homers and 30 stolen bases.

Sosa donated 250 computers to schools in the Dominican Republic, and, when the city of San Pedro de Macoris needed an ambulance, he financed that.

"I'll never forget where I came from," Sosa said. "I'm proud of the United States. They've given me everything that I have. They gave me the opportunity to be Sammy Sosa today. But I have to remember that these are my people, people I have to take care of, people I have to give jobs to when I open the plaza. This is my life."

In the center of 30-30 Plaza is a fountain with a statue of Sosa. It is the Fuente de los Limpia Botas, the Fountain of the Shoeshine Boys. Sammy Sosa once shined shoes in the Parque Duarte in the center of town. He has never forgotten his roots or his humble beginnings. All money thrown into the fountain goes toward helping the shoeshine boys in San Pedro de Macoris.

"He was always grateful, even if it was a peso," said Bill Chase, for whom Sosa once shined shoes. Chase switched roles as Sammy became successful and helped him run the Sammy Sosa Charitable Foundation, which was established in 1998.

Chase has watched Sammy mature from a shoeshine boy hustling for pesos in the street to a smart businessman worth millions of dollars. "He amazes me," Chase said of Sosa. "He hasn't changed as a person. He's got a very big heart and he's very conscientious, especially of his family."

Sosa's mother; three brothers, Luis, Juan, and Jose; and two sisters, Raquel and Sonia, are set for life because of Sammy's success in baseball. He has bought three houses for his mother, the last of which is next door to the plaza.

She is the one he salutes after each home run. Sammy touches his heart, then blows a kiss to the camera. "Para ti, mama," he says. For you, mother. In 1998, Sammy added a V symbol, which was his gesture to late Cubs broadcaster Harry Caray.

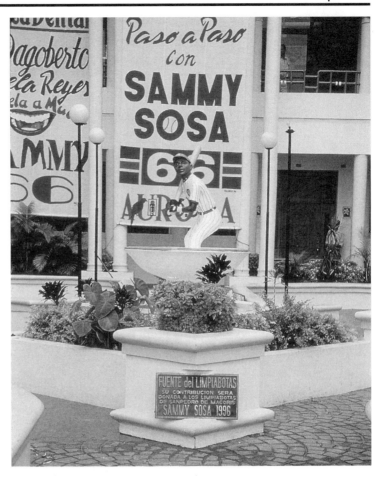

In the center of the 30–30 plaza is a fountain with a statue of Sammy Sosa. It is the fountain of the shoeshine boys, where Sammy once shined shoes as a little boy.

His brother Juan spends most of the baseball season with Sammy and his family in Chicago, acting as an unofficial bodyguard and as the babysitter for the couple's four children, Keysha, Kenia, Sammy Jr., and Michael. Juan also has seen his little brother grow up in an admirable way. "He's matured a lot, and he's changed for the better, not for the worse," Juan said.

The $42.5 million contract the Cubs gave Sosa in 1997 could have changed him for the worse. Sammy could have become lazy, but instead he worked even harder. His

*Sammy and his mother
Lucrecia*

numbers back him up—66 home runs, a league-leading 158 RBIs, and a career-best .308 batting average in 1998. "That's why he hustled this year—to show people he's worth the money," Juan said of the incredible season.

Sammy has an unofficial fan club in right field that salaams him every time he runs onto the field to take his position. In 1997, he started Sammy's Super Sundays for Cubs home games. For these games, Sosa donates 50 tickets to underprivileged children. He celebrated the first Super Sunday on May 18, 1997, with two home runs and a Cubs win. Before the game, which also was a Beanie Baby giveaway for the first 10,000 kids, Sammy jumped on top of the Cubs' dugout and signed autographs in an impromptu session.

In December 1997, Sammy embarked on a seven-city "Sammy Claus" tour, in which he distributed more than 7,000 gifts to children in schools and hospitals. The tour made stops in Washington, D.C., Philadelphia, New York, Chicago, Miami, San Pedro de Macoris, and Santo Domingo. Sammy really got into the spirit of the season. He posed in a Santa Claus suit in a photo session for *Baseball Weekly* magazine in Washington, D.C., and liked the bright red outfit so much, he rented it for the rest of his tour.

Sammy and his daughters Keysha and Kenia in front of a painting of Sammy

In 1998, hurricane Georges left destruction everywhere in the Dominican Republic. Sammy dedicated himself to helping the people of the island rebuild.

But Sosa's biggest challenge came in 1998 when Hurricane Georges ravaged the Dominican Republic in late September. Hundreds of thousands of people were left homeless, and Sosa dedicated himself to helping them rebuild. When the Cubs were in Houston for the last weekend of the regular season, Sosa and his teammates and countrymen Henry Rodriguez and Manny Alexander went to the Dominican Republic consulate to help load trucks with food and emergency supplies. The consulate had called Sosa early September 26 to ask if he could assist in the efforts. "I said, 'I'm there,'" Sammy said. The Cubs donated

$50,000 to Sosa's foundation, Gatorade sent a check for $21,000, and Chicago city officials collected $8,600. Thousands of checks arrived at Wrigley Field in response to his plea for help.

After the 1998 baseball season, Sosa returned to the Dominican Republic to a hero's welcome.

Major League Baseball made a $1 million donation to the American Red Cross Disaster Relief Fund for the Dominican Republic and Puerto Rico to help the countries recover from the hurricane. Sammy was deeply touched by the outpouring of support for his countrymen.

When he finally returned to his homeland on October 20, Sosa received a hero's welcome. Leonel Fernandez, president of the Dominican Republic, greeted Sammy, as did Juan Marichal, the director of sports for the country. That was the official red carpet treatment. Sosa and his family drove from the capital city of Santo Domingo to his hometown of San Pedro de Macoris, where thousands cheered his return.

Sammy Sosa is one of the most well known people in the Dominican Republic. People everywhere follow his baseball career.

"Bienvenido a tu pais, Sammy," read signs everywhere. Welcome to your country.

His 66 home runs not only captured the attention of baseball fans in the United States, but they gave people in his homeland something to cheer about. He gave them hope.

"I always say, he was chosen by God," his brother Juan said.

During Sammy's postgame news conference on Sammy Sosa Day, September 20, 1998, someone asked him about his next goal in life.

"Go to heaven," Sammy said.

It is a good goal to have.

CHRONOLOGY

1968   Born November 12, in San Pedro de Macoris, Dominican Republic

1985   Signed first professional contract with Texas Rangers, July 30, at age of 16

1986   Made his professional debut with Gulf Coast Rookie League team

1989   Made his major-league debut for the Texas Rangers on June 16, against the New York Yankees, going 2 for 4; hit his first major-league home run June 21 off Boston's Roger Clemens Traded July 29, to the Chicago White Sox with pitcher Wilson Alvarez and infielder Scott Fletcher for outfielder Harold Baines and infielder Fred Manrique; made his White Sox debut August 22, at Minnesota and went 3 for 3 with a homer and 2 RBIs

1991   Married Sonia Esther in Santo Domingo, Dominican Republic, in November

1992   Traded March 30, to Chicago Cubs with pitcher Ken Patterson for outfielder George Bell

1993   Became the first player in Cubs history to record a 30-homer, 30-stolen-base season; finished with 33 homers and 36 stolen bases

1995   Repeated the 30-30 feat, hitting 36 homers and stealing 34 bases; named to the 1995 National League All-Star team for the first time and went 0 for 1 in the game at Texas

1996   Had 40 homers by August 20, when he was hit by a pitch by Florida's Mark Hutton and suffered broken right hand

1997   Hit his 200th major-league home run August 24, off Montreal's Steve Kline

1998   Hit 20 home runs in June to set a major-league single-month record; previous mark was 18 set by Detroit's Rudy York in August 1937; hit first career grand slam July 27, off Arizona's Alan Embree, and hit his second the next day, also at Arizona; hit home run No. 56 on September 2, to tie Hack Wilson's 1930 National League record; hit home run No. 60 on September 12, to tie Babe Ruth's 1927 record; hit home run No. 61 on September 13, to tie Roger Maris' 1961 record; the Chicago Cubs celebrate Sammy Sosa Day on September 20, at Wrigley Field; finished the 1998 season with 66 home runs, hitting his last off Houston's Jose Lima on September 25; won NL MVP award in November

1998 HOME RUNS

No.	Date	Opponent	Pitcher	Distance	Result
1	4/4	vs. Mon	Marc Valdes	371	Cubs, 3-1
2	4/11	at Mon	Anthony Telford	350	Expos, 5-4 (10)
3	4/15	at NYMets	Dennis Cook	430	Mets, 2-1
4	4/23	vs. SD	Dan Miceli	420	Padres, 4-1
5	4/24	at LA	Ismael Valdes	430	Dodgers, 12-4
6	4/27	at SD	Joey Hamilton	434	Cubs, 3-1
7	5/3	vs. StL	Cliff Politte	370	Cardinals, 8-5
8	5/16	at Cin	Scott Sullivan	420	Cubs, 5-4
9	5/22	at Atl	Greg Maddux	440	Braves, 8-2
10	5/25	at Atl	Kevin Millwood	410	Braves, 9-5
11	5/25	at Atl	Mike Cather	420	Braves, 9-5
12	5/27	vs. Phi	Darrin Winston	460	Phillies, 10-5
13	5/27	vs. Phi	Wayne Gomes	400	Phillies, 10-5
14	6/1	vs. Fla	Ryan Dempster	430	Cubs, 10-2
15	6/1	vs. Fla	Oscar Hernandez	410	Cubs, 10-2
16	6/3	vs. Fla	Livan Hernandez	370	Cubs, 5-1
17	6/5	vs. ChiSox	Jim Parque	370	Cubs, 6-5 (12)
18	6/6	vs. ChiSox	Carlos Castillo	410	Cubs, 7-6
19	6/7	vs. ChiSox	James Baldwin	380	Cubs, 13-7
20	6/8	vs. Min	LaTroy Hawkins	340	Cubs, 8-1
21	6/13	at Phi	Mark Portugal	350	Cubs, 10-8 (10)
22	6/15	vs. Mil	Cal Eldred	420	Cubs, 6-5
23	6/15	vs. Mil	Cal Eldred	410	Cubs, 6-5
24	6/15	vs. Mil	Cal Eldred	415	Cubs, 6-5
25	6/17	vs. Mil	Bronswell Patrick	430	Brewers, 6-5
26	6/19	vs. Phi	Carlton Loewer	380	Phillies, 9-8 (12)
27	6/19	vs. Phi	Carlton Loewer	380	Phillies, 9-8 (12)
28	6/20	vs. Phi	Matt Beech	366	Cubs, 9-4
29	6/20	vs. Phi	Toby Borland	500	Cubs, 9-4
30	6/21	vs. Phi	Tyler Green	380	Phillies, 7-2
31	6/24	at Det	Seth Greisinger	390	Tigers, 7-6 (11)
32	6/25	at Det	Brian Moehler	400	Tigers, 6-4
33	6/30	vs. Ari	Alan Embree	364	Diamondbacks, 7-4
34	7/9	at Mil	Jeff Juden	430	Brewers, 12-9
35	7/10	at Mil	Scott Karl	450	Brewers, 6-5
36	7/17	at Fla	Kirt Ojala	440	Cubs, 6-1

No.	Date	Opponent	Pitcher	Distance	Result
37	7/22	vs. Mon	Miguel Batista	365	Cubs, 9-5
38	7/26	vs. NYMets	Rick Reed	420	Cubs, 3-1
39	7/27	at Ari	Willie Blair	350	Cubs, 6-2
40	7/27	at Ari	Alan Embree	420	Cubs, 6-2
41	7/28	at Ari	Bob Wolcott	400	Diamondbacks, 7-5
42	7/31	vs. Col	Jamey Wright	380	Cubs, 9-1
43	8/5	vs. Ari	Andy Benes	380	Diamondbacks, 10-7
44	8/8	at StL	Rich Croushore	400	Cardinals, 9-8 (13)
45	8/10	at SF	Russ Ortiz	370	Cubs, 8-5
46	8/10	at SF	Chris Brock	420	Cubs, 8-5
47	8/16	at Hou	Sean Bergman	360	Cubs, 2-1 (11)
48	8/19	vs. StL	Kent Bottenfield	368	Cardinals, 8-6 (10)
49	8/21	vs. SF	Orel Hershiser	430	Cubs, 6-5
50	8/23	vs. Hou	Jose Lima	433	Astros, 13-3
51	8/23	vs. Hou	Jose Lima	388	Astros, 13-3
52	8/26	at Cin	Brett Tomko	440	Cubs, 9-2
53	8/28	at Col	John Thomson	414	Cubs, 10-5
54	8/30	at Col	Darryl Kile	482	Cubs, 4-3
55	8/31	vs. Cin	Brett Tomko	364	Cubs, 5-4
56	9/2	vs. Cin	Jason Bere	370	Cubs, 4-2
57	9/4	at Pit	Jason Schmidt	400	Cubs, 8-4
58	9/5	at Pit	Sean Lawrence	405	Pirates, 4-3
59	9/11	vs. Mil	Bill Pulsipher	433	Brewers, 13-11
60	9/12	vs. Mil	Valerio De Los Santos	390	Cubs, 15-12
61	9/13	vs. Mil	Bronswell Patrick	480	Cubs, 11-10 (10)
62	9/13	vs. Mil	Eric Plunk	480	Cubs, 11-10 (10)
63	9/16	at SD	Brian Boehringer	434	Cubs, 6-3
64	9/23	at Mil	Rafael Roque	344	Brewers, 8-7
65	9/23	at Mil	Rod Henderson	410	Brewers, 8-7
66	9/25	at Hou	Jose Lima	420	Astros, 6-2

MAJOR LEAGUE STATS

YR	TEAM	G	AB	R	H	2B	3B	HR	RBI	BB	AVG
1989	2TM	58	183	27	47	8	0	4	13	11	.257
	Tex	25	84	8	20	3	0	1	3	0	.238
	ChA	33	99	19	27	5	0	3	10	11	.273
1990	ChA	153	532	72	124	26	10	15	70	33	.233
1991	ChA	116	316	39	64	10	1	10	33	14	.203
1992	ChN	67	262	41	68	7	2	8	25	19	.260
1993	ChN	159	598	92	156	25	5	33	93	38	.261
1994	ChN	105	426	59	128	17	6	25	70	25	.300
1995	ChN	144	564	89	151	17	3	36	119	58	.268
1996	ChN	124	498	84	136	21	2	40	100	34	.273
1997	ChN	162	642	90	161	31	4	36	119	45	.251
1998	ChN	159	643	134	198	20	0	66	158	73	.308
TOTALS		1247	4664	727	1233	182	33	273	800	350	.264

INDEX